Water! Water!
A Kid's Guide To Amsterdam, Netherlands

Photography by John D. Weigand
Poetry by Penelope Dyan

Bellissima Publishing, LLC
Jamul, California
www.bellissimapublishing.com

Copyright © 2015 by Penny D. Weigand and John D. Weigand

All rights reserved. No part of this book may be reproduced or transmitted in any form or by any means, electronic or mechanical, including photocopying, recording, or by any other means, or by any information or storage retrieval system, without permission from the publisher.

ISBN 978-1-61477-189-0
First Edition

"Water is the driving force of all nature."

Leonardo da Vinci

Water! Water!
Bellissima Publishing, LLC

Introduction

Amsterdam, Netherlands (Holland) has more museums than any other city in the world! But if you ask a kid, most kids really don't like museums and stuff like that much, unless it happens to be a place for Kids, like the Nemo Science Center--yes, that's right, Nemo, like the fish! And you can even take a tour boat to get there for a fun hands on science experience! Some of the other museums you can see are the Anne Frank Museum, the Van Gogh Museum (the guy who cut off his ear) and Rijksmuseum, just to name a few. People get around Amsterdam by bike, by bus and by boat, and sometimes by car. You can take a hop on hop off bus, or you can take a hop on hop off boat; and (of course) taking a boat ride is always loads of fun for kids.

When you travel anywhere, the main thing you want to do is feel the city; and award winning author, attorney and former teacher, Penelope Dyan and talented photographer, John D. Weigand, do just that! This 'learn to read' book with its extra large print is the perfect size to take along in a kid's backpack, and Dysn and Weigand have a knack of spotting things a child likes to see! This, coupled with the free music video on the Bellissimavideo YouTube Channel, makes learning fun! And learning should always be fun!

Water! Water!
Bellissima Publishing, LLC

Water! Water!
A Kid's Guide To Amsterdam, Netherlands

Photography by John D. Weigand
Poetry by Penelope Dyan

There are canals and bridges
just everywhere look,
and Amsterdam is NOTHING like
what you READ in that book.
And For you, I have a bit of news.
People do NOT clomp around
in big wooden shoes.

But you can get around
quite easily on a boat.
And through ALL those canals
you can EASILY float.

First, you see one boat.
And then you see two!
There are big boats.
There are small boats.
And there's a WHOLE lot to do!

You can look through this bridge and then you can float through. You can ride a bike over this bridge. It's ALL up to you!

Sometimes as through
the canals you go,
you can even see TWO bridges
right in a row!

With bicycles parked above,
as under you float,
you see a house parked ahead of you
that's REALLY a boat!
And above the bridge,
and on the right,
are rows of tall, narrow houses
that will soon light up the night.

Over this bridge you can walk,
and with Mom and Dad
you can talk and talk!

There are more houses
and lots of cars parked on the street.
The guide says, "The houses,
are narrow, deep, tall and NOT wide."
And YOU think THAT is neat!
He says the narrower the house
was from the front,
the less tax people had to pay.
And so THAT is WHY the houses
were built that way!
He says the fronts of the houses
appear to hide
how really BIG they ARE
when you go inside!

The Nemo Science Center
is a fun place to be,
You can have fun at six years of age,
or at the age of ninety-three!
You can pretend to be a scientist,
and learn lots of stuff;
and you can just hang around
until you've seen and learned enough.
But before you take off
to go anywhere,
at this water clock,
you will stop and you will stare.

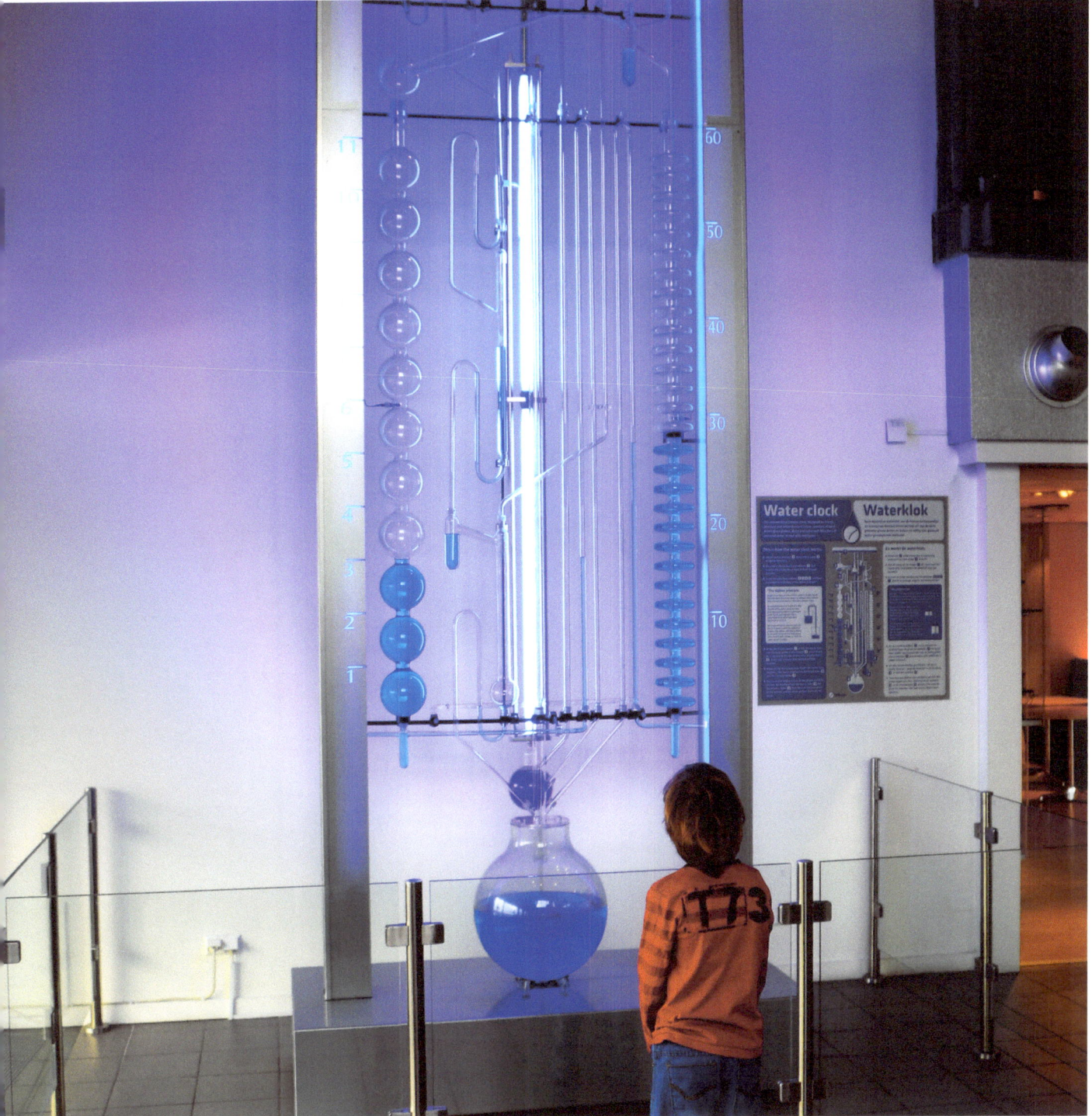

You get back on your tour boat, and what happens to you? The bridge overhead splits right into two!

And then you are there!
Anne Frank's family's house is ahead!
To the left of their home
is an awning of red.
Anne wanted to be a writer,
and so she wrote everyday.
She wrote about World War II,
and why their family hid away.
You, see as impossible as it did seem,
to be a writer was her dream.
And although she sadly died
after being taken cruelly away,
the words she wrote then,
you can still read today!

And finally as dusk turns into night,
the Basilica of St. Nicholas
stands shining bright!
And you think of Anne Frank
who so long ago,
left an important message,
the world needed to know.
And you vow to remember
the lessons she told,
for all of your years, until you are old.
Anne's story was of selfless love,
of hope, and a dream.
She had a courage of heart
few have or have seen.

"The crowning fortune of a man is to be born to some pursuit which finds him employment and happiness, whether it be to make baskets, or broadswords, or canals, or statues, or songs."

Ralph Waldo Emerson

www.ingramcontent.com/pod-product-compliance
Ingram Content Group UK Ltd.
Pitfield, Milton Keynes, MK11 3LW, UK
UKHW060135240426
12048UKWH00002B/51